Read   Trace   Write

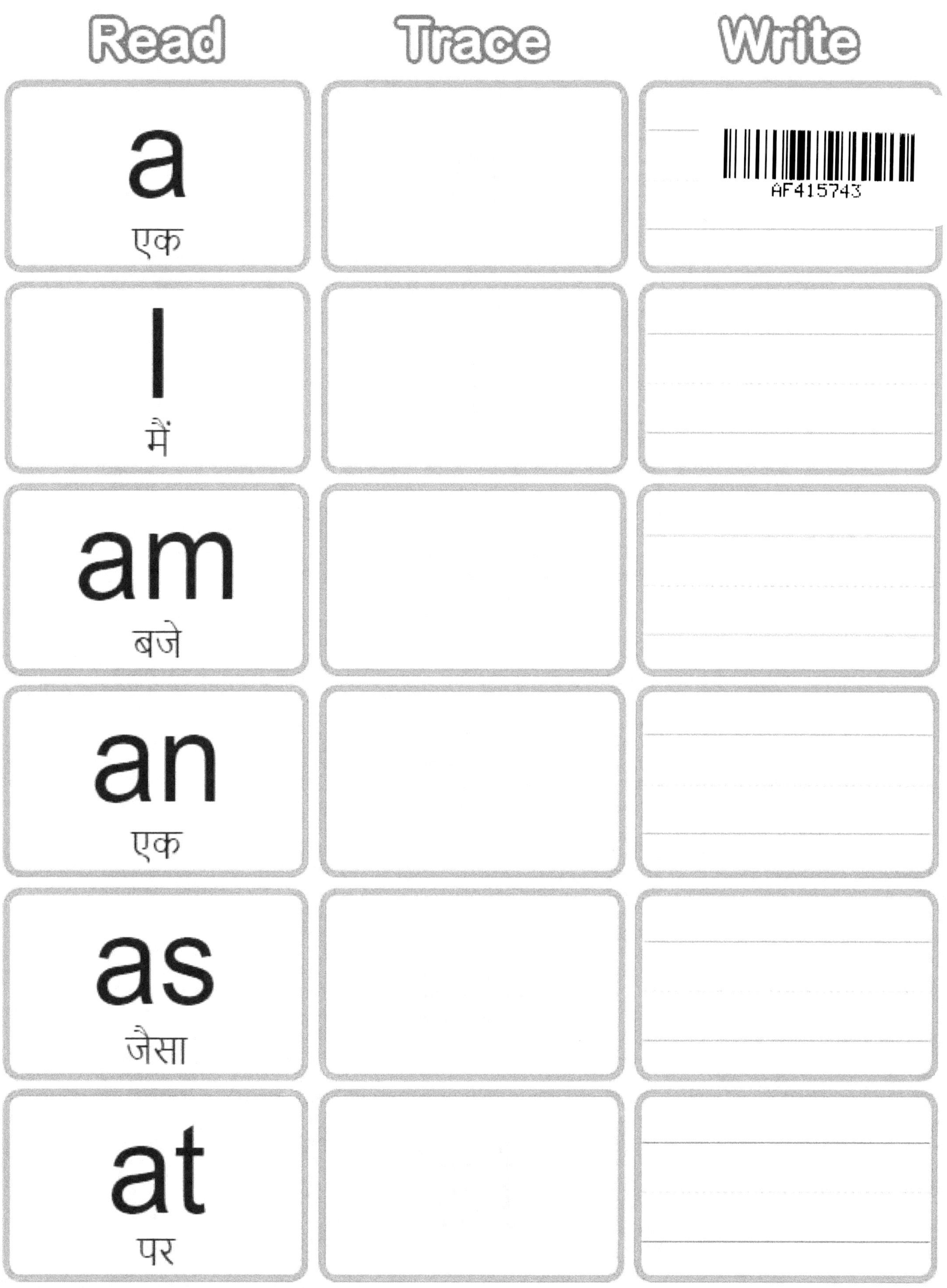

Read and write the sentence!

a		This is a bird.
I		I will play with the toys.
am		I am crawling on the ground.
an		This is an ant.
as		It is as light as a feather.
at		She is at her friend's house.

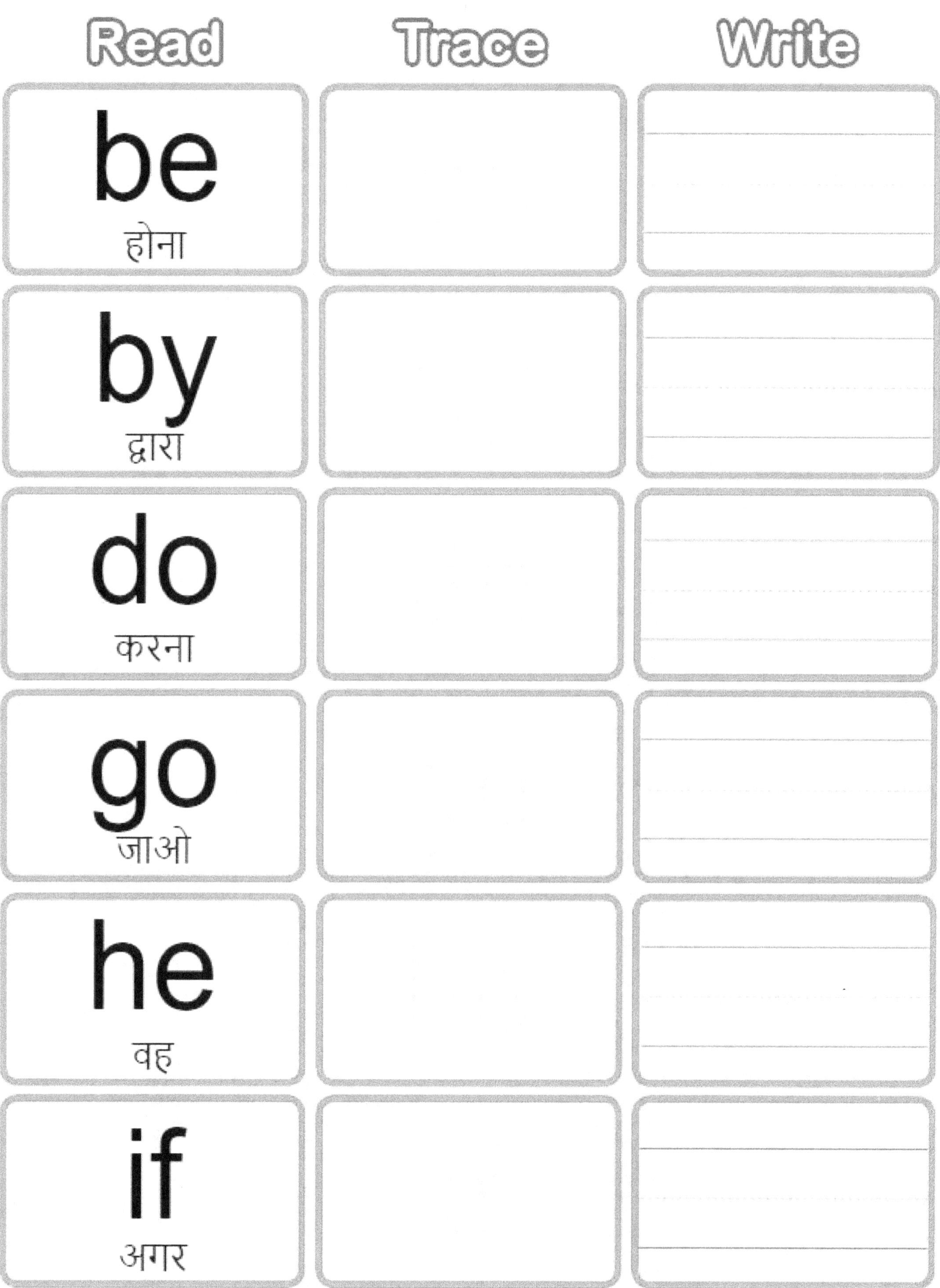

Read
Trace
Write
be
होना
by
द्वारा
do
करना
go
जाओ
he
वह
if
अगर

Read and write the sentence!

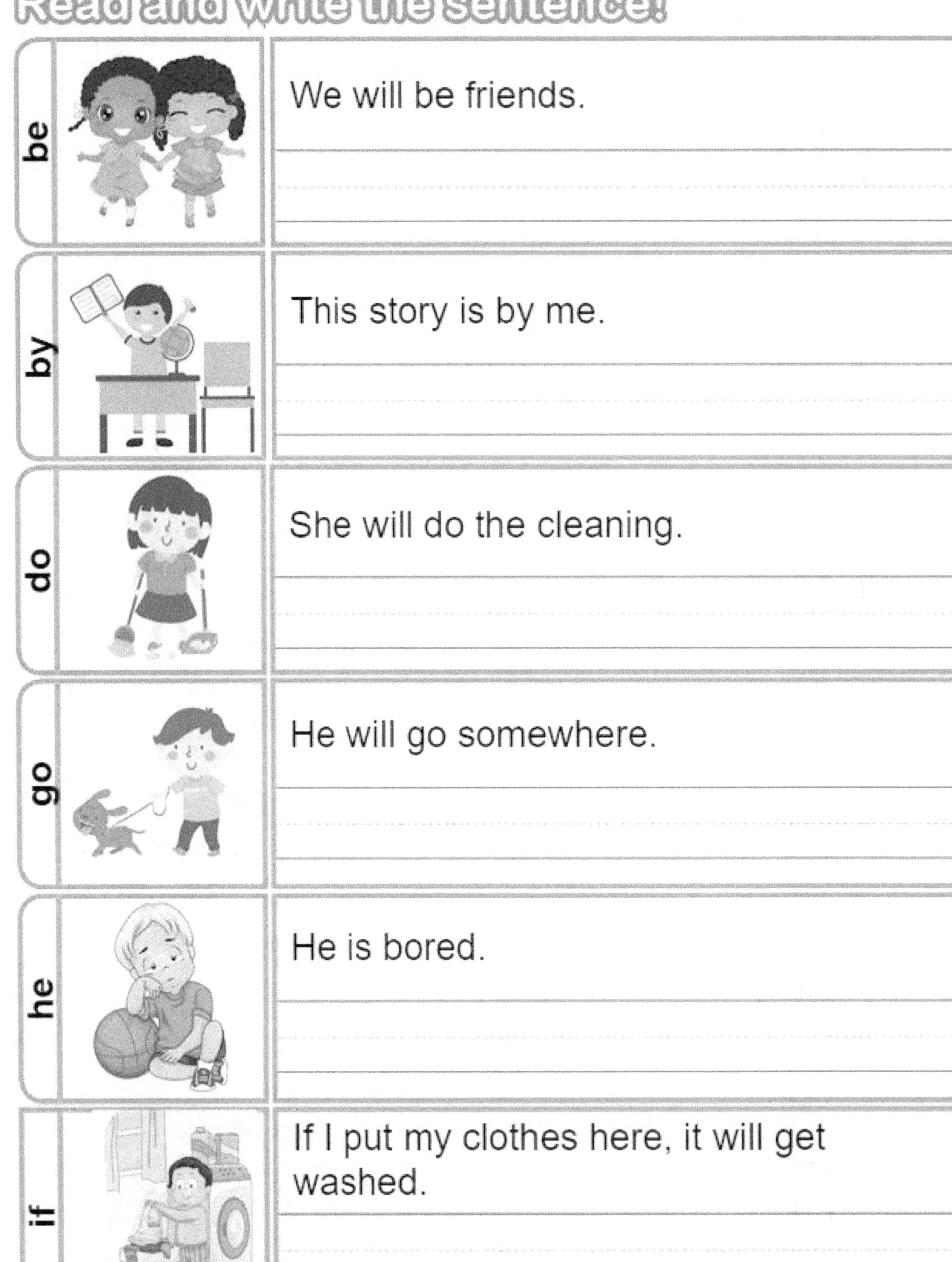

be		We will be friends.
by		This story is by me.
do		She will do the cleaning.
go		He will go somewhere.
he		He is bored.
if		If I put my clothes here, it will get washed.

Read   Trace   Write

Read and write the sentence!

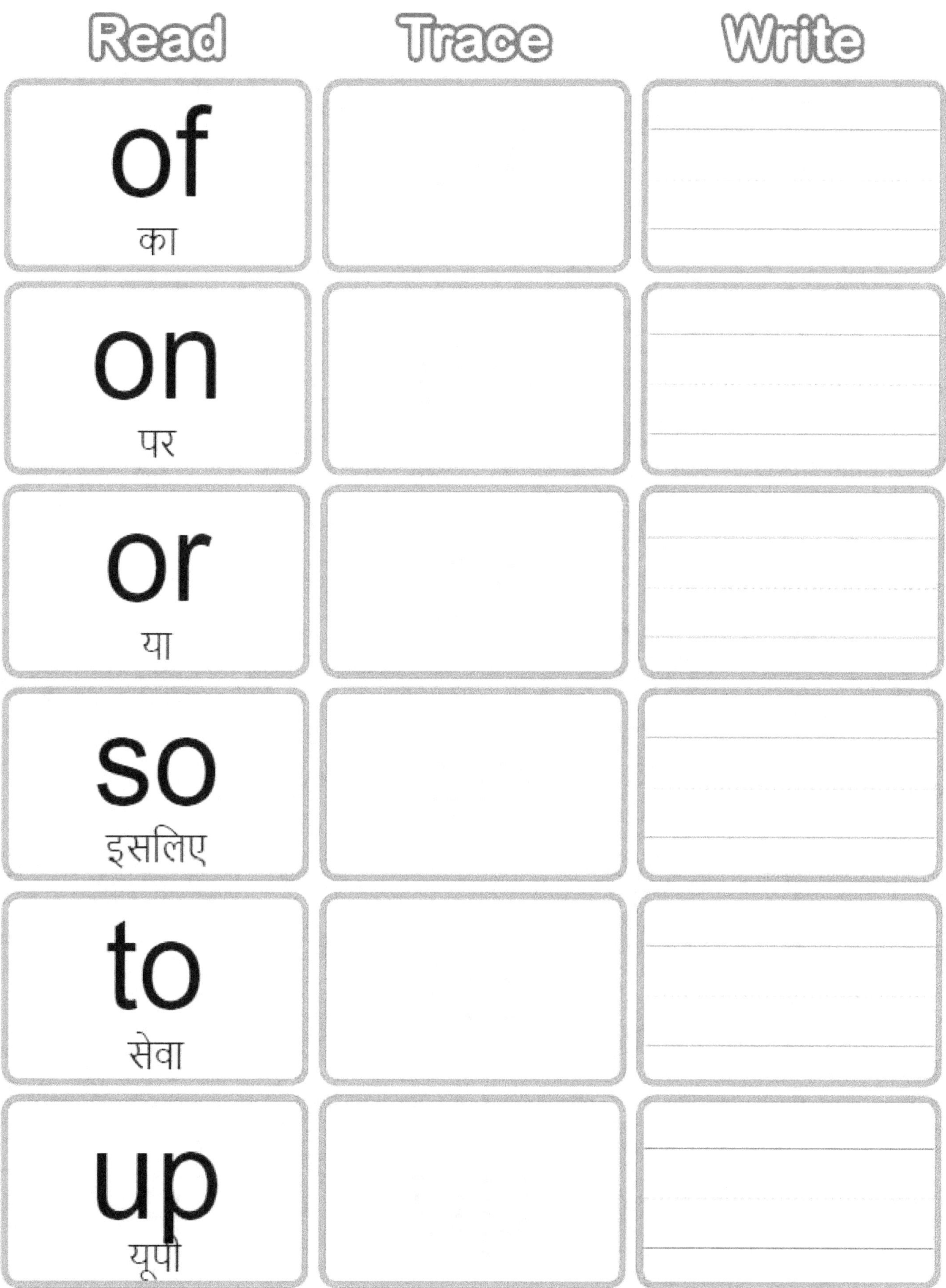

Read	Trace	Write
of का		
on पर		
or या		
so इसलिए		
to सेवा		
up यूपी		

Read and write the sentence!

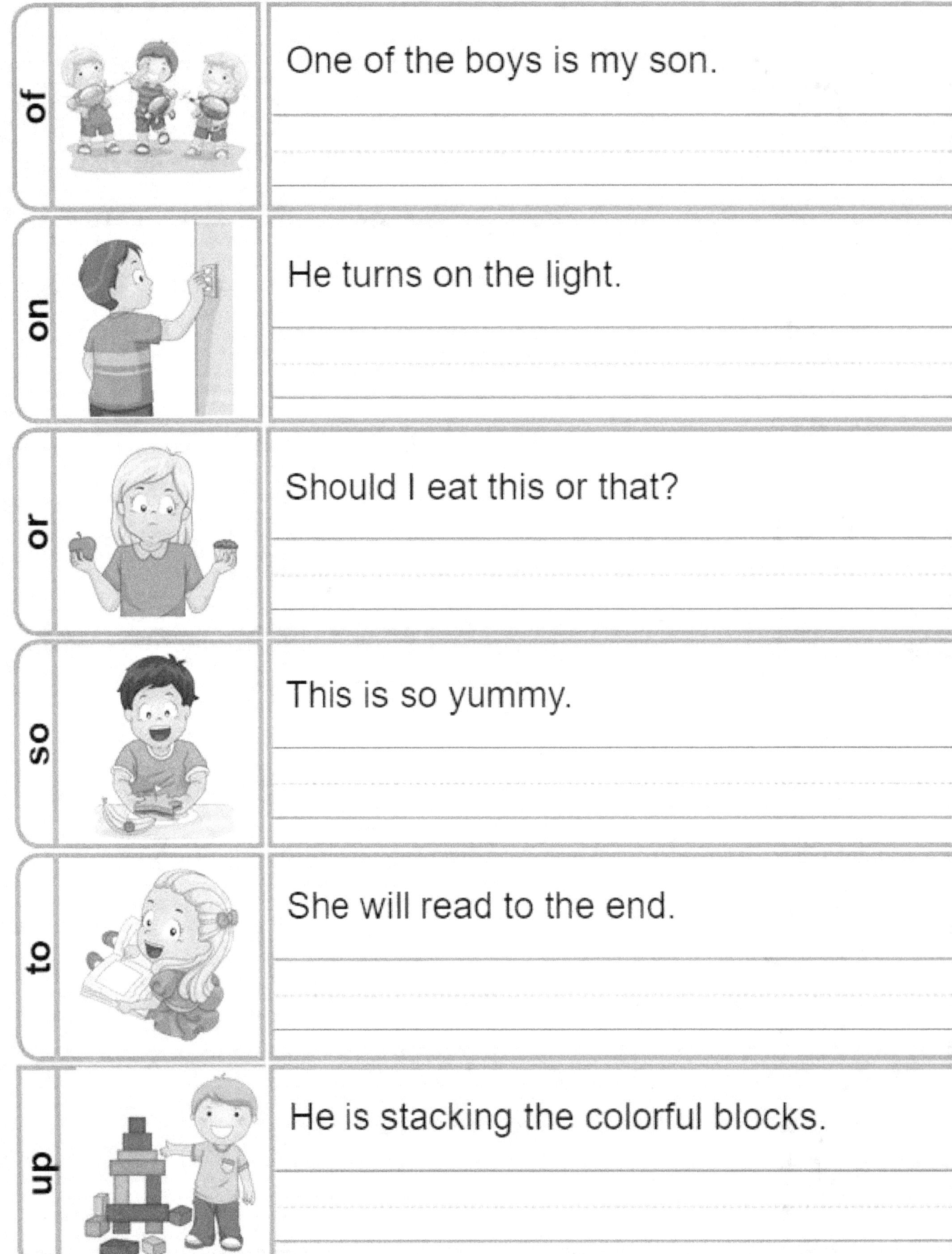

Read	Trace	Write
us हमें		
we हम		
all सब		
and तथा		
any कोई भी		
are कर रहे हैं		

Read and write the sentence!

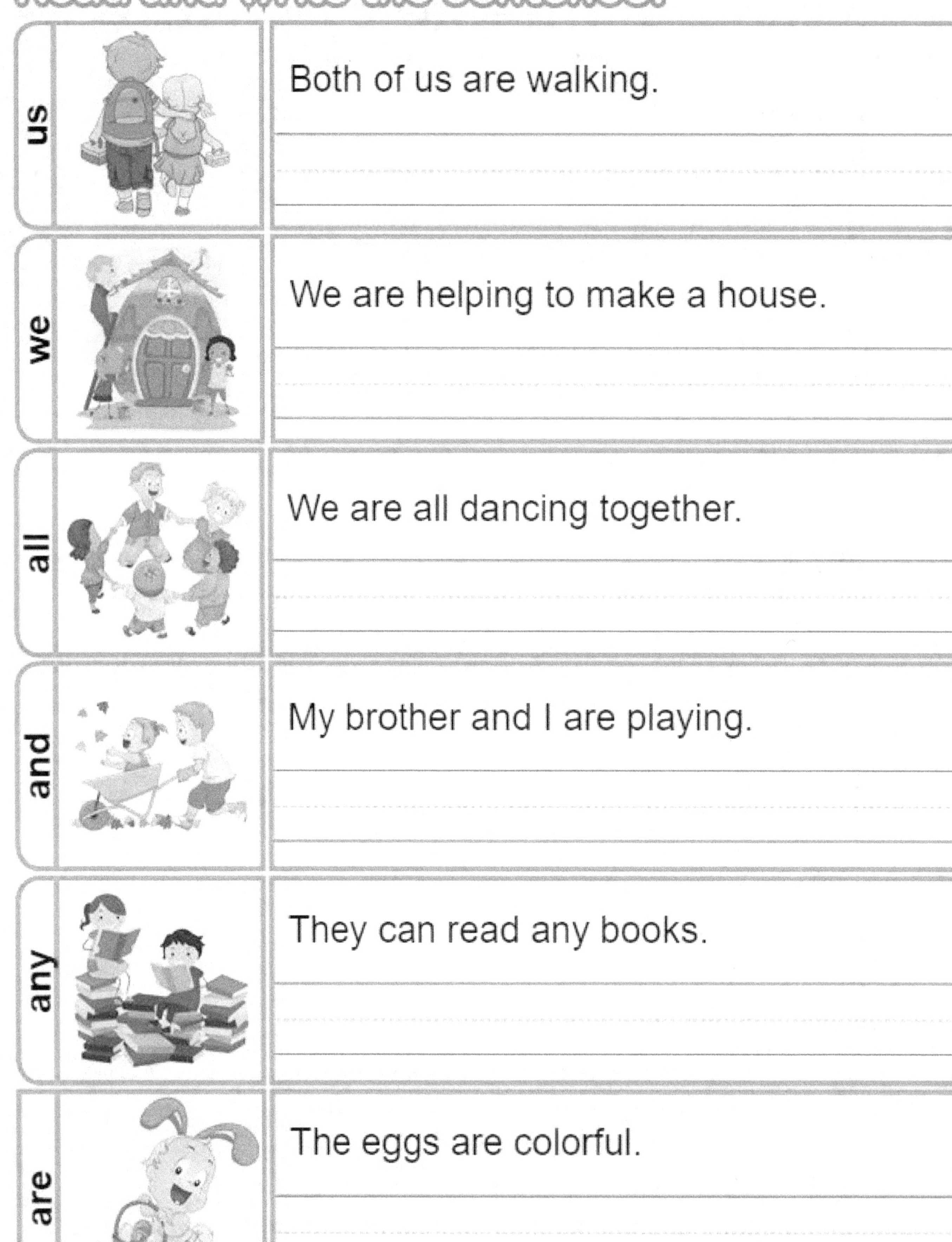

Read
Trace
Write
ask
पूछना
ate
खाया
bed
बिस्तर
big
बड़े
box
डिब्बा
boy
लड़का

Read and write the sentence!

	Sentence
ask	The girl asks a question.
ate	They ate yummy ice cream.
bed	This bed is for the baby.
big	The bottle is very big.
box	The box has all my toys.
boy	The boy is hiding behind it.

Read
Trace
Write
but
परंतु
buy
खरीद
can
कर सकते हैं
car
गाड़ी
cat
बिल्ली
cow
गाय

but		I want to go, but my son doesn't.
buy		He buys lots of stuff.
can		The baby will drink milk from the can.
car		The car is red.
cat		The cat is sad.
cow		The cow is funny.

Read
Trace
Write
cut
कट गया
day
दिन
did
किया
dog
कुत्ता
eat
खा
egg
अंडा

Read and write the sentence!

Read
Trace
Write
eye
आंख
far
दूर
fly
उड़ना
for
के लिये
get
प्राप्त
got
गॉट

Read and write the sentence!

Read	Trace	Write
had था		
has है		
her उसके		
him उसे		
his उसके		
hot गरम		

Read and write the sentence!

had	He had a big tummy.
has	She has a doll.
her	She has her trolley.
him	I gave my hat to him.
his	His cheeks are big.
hot	It is hot on the beach.

Read
Trace
Write
how
किस तरह
its
आईटी इस
leg
टांग
let
चलो
man
आदमी
may
हो सकता है

how

How many blocks are there?

its

Its legs are short.

leg

His legs are short.

let

Let me come in!

man

The man is a vet.

may

May I have more?

<table>
<tr><th>Read</th><th>Trace</th><th>Write</th></tr>
<tr><td>men
पुरुषों</td><td></td><td></td></tr>
<tr><td>new
नया</td><td></td><td></td></tr>
<tr><td>not
नहीं</td><td></td><td></td></tr>
<tr><td>now
अभी</td><td></td><td></td></tr>
<tr><td>off
बंद</td><td></td><td></td></tr>
<tr><td>old
पुराना</td><td></td><td></td></tr>
</table>

Read and write the sentence!

men — The men are mining for gold.

new — She has a new hat.

not — She is not feeling well.

now — Now I am doing my homework.

off — They cut off the paper.

old — You are one year old!

Read	Trace	Write

one
एक

our
हमारी

out
बाहर

own
अपना

pig
सूअर

put
डाल

Read and write the sentence!

one	The panda says one.
our	This is our room.
out	He will go out.
own	The man owns a computer.
pig	She is sleeping on her pig.
put	She is putting an arm around her daughter.

Read	Trace	Write

ran
daud

red
लाल

run
daud

saw
देख

say
कहते हैं

see
देख

Read and write the sentence!

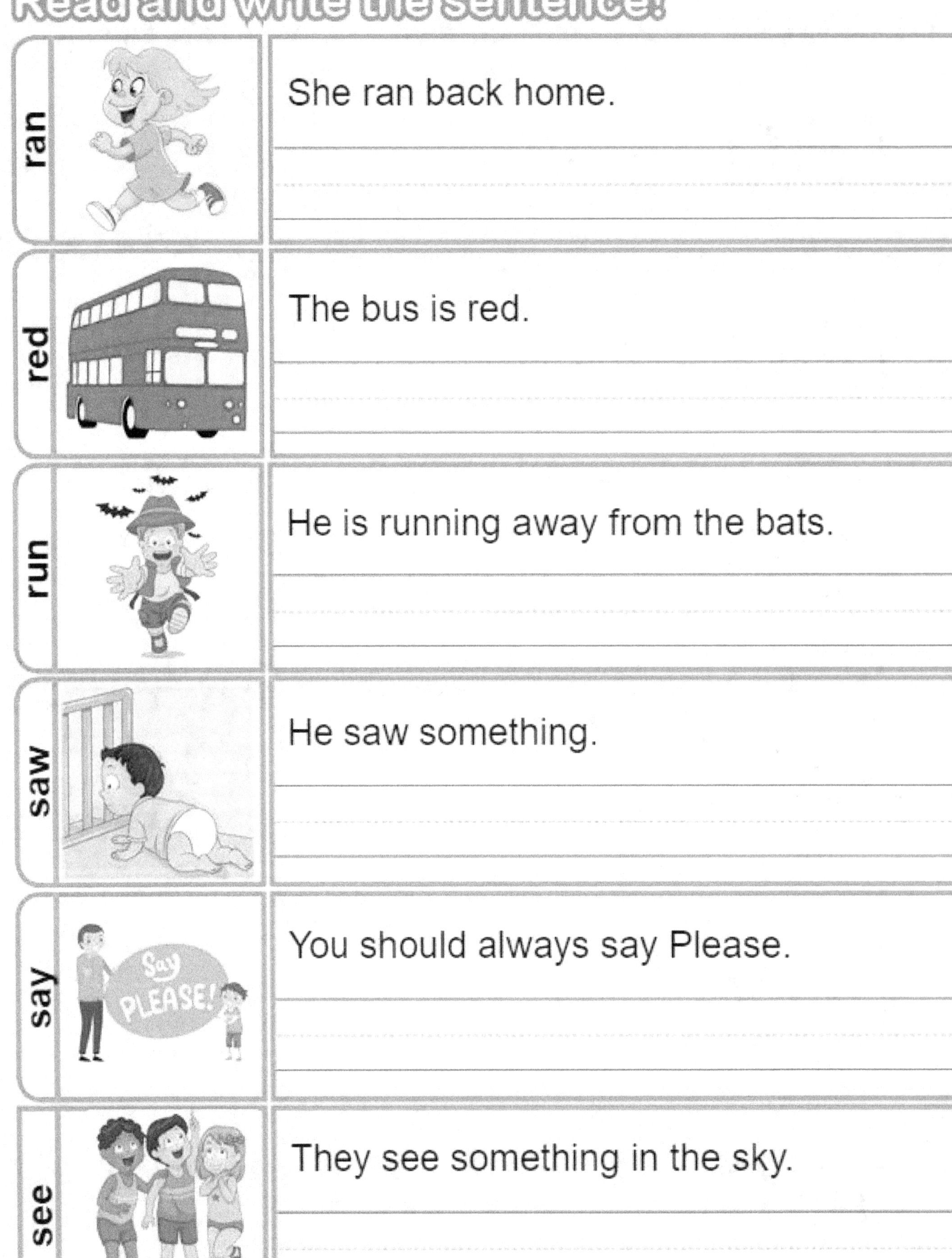

Read
Trace
Write
she
वह
sit
बैठिये
six
छह
sun
रवि
ten
दस
the
एक

Read and write the sentence!

she	She is smiling.
sit	The baby is sitting.
six	Number six is my lucky number.
sun	The sun is shining.
ten	The monkey can count to ten.
the	The baby is playing with the ball.

Read	Trace	Write
too बहुत		
top ऊपर		
toy खिलौना		
try प्रयत्न		
two दो		
use उपयोग		

Read and write the sentence!

	Sentence
too	The bear is too cute.
top	The pot is on the top.
toy	The baby has lots of toys.
try	We try to be kind to him.
two	Today you have turned two.
use	I use my toothpaste and toothbrush.

Read
Trace
Write
was
था
way
मार्ग
who
क्या
why
क्यों
yes
हाँ
you
आप

Read and write the sentence!

was	He was reading a book.
way	Let's go this way
who	Who wants to dance?
why	Why is the machine not working?
yes	Yes, I am so happy!
you	I love you!

Read	Trace	Write
away दूर		
baby बच्चा		
back वापस		
ball गेंद		
bear भालू		
been था		

Read and write the sentence!

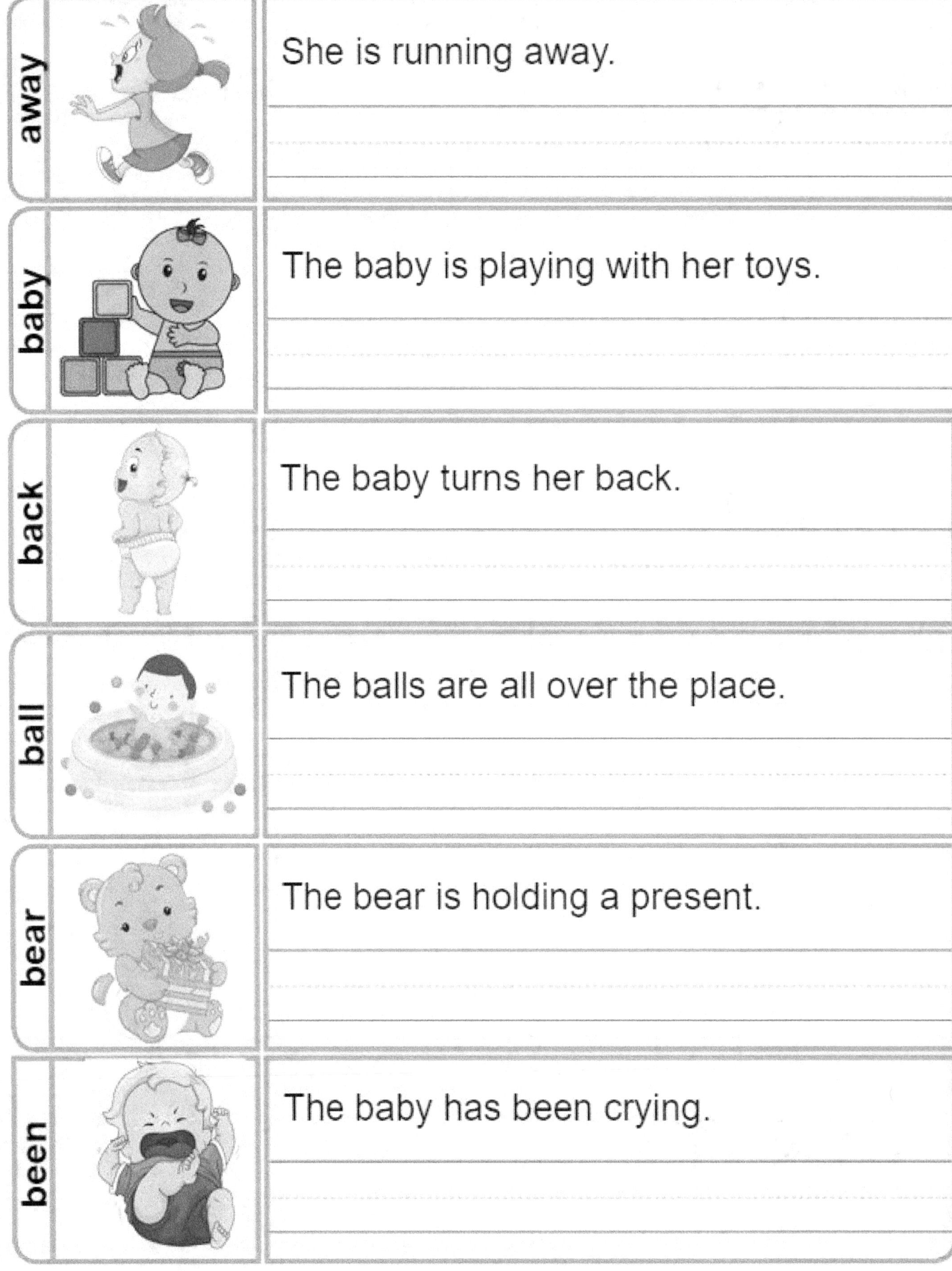

away		She is running away.
baby		The baby is playing with her toys.
back		The baby turns her back.
ball		The balls are all over the place.
bear		The bear is holding a present.
been		The baby has been crying.

Read
Trace
Write
bell
घंटी
best
श्रेष्ठ
bird
चिड़िया
blue
नीला
boat
नाव
both
दोनों

Read and write the sentence!

bell		The bells are ringing.
best		This is the best food for babies.
bird		The bird is flying.
blue		The boy dressed up in blue.
boat		The boat will go into the ocean.
both		Both of you look so much alike.

Read
Trace
Write
cake
केक
call
कॉल
came
आया
coat
कोट
cold
सर्दी
come
आइए

Read and write the sentence!

cake		The cake is for your birthday.
call		She is calling for somebody.
came		She came with her bag.
coat		The girl is wearing her coat.
cold		The baby feels cold.
come		Come here to the slide!

Read	Trace	Write
corn मक्का		
does कर देता है		
doll गुड़िया		
done किया हुआ		
door द्वार		
down नीचे		

Read and write the sentence!

corn	The corn tastes good.
does	Does that thing taste bad?
doll	She is hugging her doll.
done	I've done reading my book.
door	They open the door.
down	The boy turns his head down.

Read	Trace	Write
draw खींचना		
duck बत्तख		
fall गिरना		
farm खेत		
fast तेज		
feet पैर		

Read and write the sentence!

draw	They all draw pictures.
duck	The duck is yellow.
fall	He fell down from the swing.
farm	He grows crops at his farm.
fast	She is doing everything very fast.
feet	I touch my feet.

Read
Trace
Write
find
खोज
fire
आग
fish
मछली
five
पांच
four
चार
from
से

Read and write the sentence!

find	 They are finding something.
fire	 The fire is blazing and dangerous.
fish	 The fish are swimming in the ocean.
five	 You get birthday gifts for turning five.
four	 The lion is turning four today.
from	 She will draw a picture of her flower.

Read	Trace	Write
full पूर्ण		
game खेल		
gave दिया		
girl लड़की		
give देना		
goes जाता है		

Read and write the sentence!

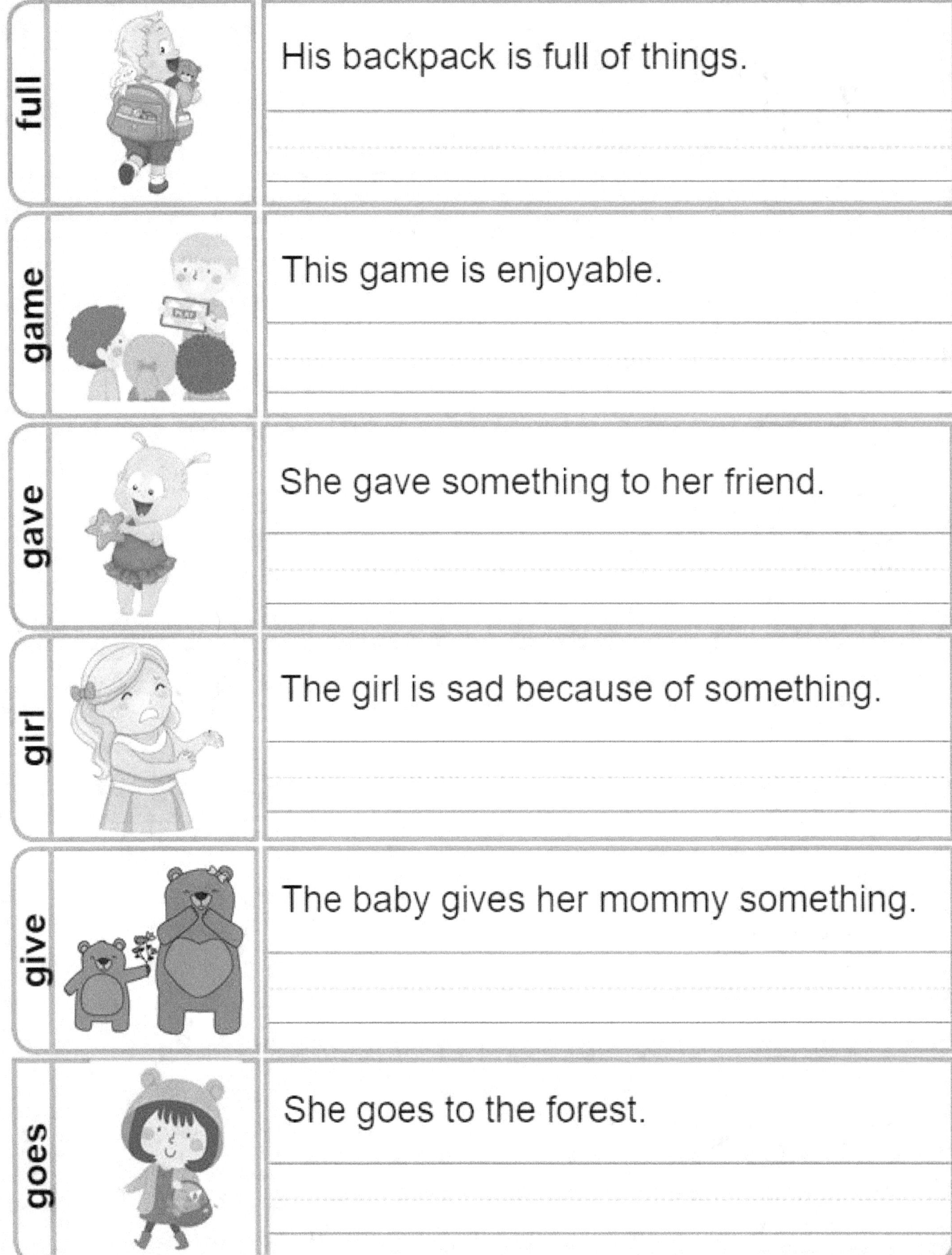

full	His backpack is full of things.
game	This game is enjoyable.
gave	She gave something to her friend.
girl	The girl is sad because of something.
give	The baby gives her mommy something.
goes	She goes to the forest.

Read
Trace
Write
good
अच्छा
grow
बढ़ना
hand
हाथ
have
है
head
सिर
help
मदद

Read and write the sentence!

good	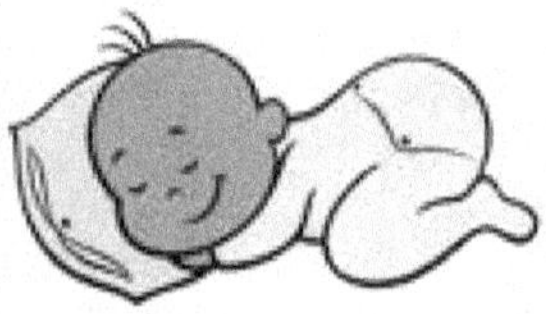	The baby is acting very well today.
grow		My plant will grow!
hand		My hand is touching the wall.
have		She will have lots of friends.
head		My head is round.
help		They help each other wash the clothes.

Read	Trace	Write
here यहाँ		
hill पहाड़ी		
hold पकड़		
home घर		
hurt चोट		
into में		

Read and write the sentence!

here	America is over here.
hill	The hill has some trees and a house.
hold	He is holding his daughter.
home	He drew a picture of his home.
hurt	The boy is hurt.
into	He will jump into the pool.

Read	Trace	Write
jump कूद		
just केवल		
keep रखना		
kind मेहरबान		
know जानना		
like पसंद		

jump — The cat jumped on the cushion.

just — The arrival of the plane just arrived.

keep — She keeps thinking about it.

kind — The woman is kind to the girl.

know — They know that they will go over there.

like — He likes to ride on the horse.

Read	Trace	Write
live लाइव		
long लंबा		
look नज़र		
made बनाया गया		
make बनाया गया		
many अनेक		

Read and write the sentence!

live

They all live together.

long

The pencil is very long.

look

They are looking at something.

made

They made a promise.

make

They are going to make something.

many

He has many shirts.

Read	Trace	Write
milk दूध		
much बहुत		
must जरूरर		
name नाम		
nest घोंसला		
once एक बार		

Read and write the sentence!

milk	I have milk for breakfast.
much	I like to eat this very much.
must	I must do all my homework.
name	My name is Joe.
nest	The bird has a nest.
once	He once liked to look at his computer.

Read
Trace
Write
only
केवल
open
खुला हुआ
over
ऊपर
pick
चुनना
play
खेल
pull
खींचें

Read and write the sentence!

only		There is only one student.
open		He wants to open the door.
over		The class is over.
pick		She picked up something.
play		They like to play together.
pull		She is pulling on her friend's hair.

Read
Trace
Write
rain
बारिश
read
पढ़ना
ride
सवारी
ring
अंगूठी
said
कहा हुआ
seed
बीज

Read and write the sentence!

rain	The rain is not going to hit us.
read	She likes to read books.
ride	The baby is riding on a toy horse.
ring	The bird is holding a ring in its beak.
said	She said hello to her neighbor.
seed	The seeds are going to plant.

SEEDS

Read	Trace	Write
shoe जूता		
show प्रदर्शन		
sing गाओ		
snow हिमपात		
some कुछ		
song गीत		

Read and write the sentence!

shoe	Her shoes are cute and purple.
show	This map shows the location.
sing	The baby can sing along.
snow	I like to play snow.
some	These are some of my toys.
song	I will sing a song in the talent show.

Read
Trace
Write
soon
जल्द ही
stop
रुकें
take
लेना
tell
कहना
that
उस
them
उन्हें

Read and write the sentence!

soon	The eggs will hatch soon.
stop	The teacher says to stop.
take	They take some flowers.
tell	She is telling a story.
that	That bird dressed up as Santa.
them	He likes to eat them.

Read
Trace
Write
then
फिर
they
वे
this
इस
time
समय
tree
पेड़
upon
के ऊपर

Read and write the sentence!

then		Then, I will go to bed.
they		They are running to school.
this		This is my duck.
time		The time always moves on.
tree		There are lots of green trees in the park.
upon		Once upon a time, there was a princess.

Read	Trace	Write
very बहुत		
walk टहल लो		
want चाहते हैं		
warm गरम		
wash धुलाई		
well कुंआ		

Read and write the sentence!

very	The baby is lovely.
walk	They are walking on the sidewalk.
want	The baby wants more milk.
warm	The bath is warm.
wash	She is going to wash the dishes.
well	He can save money well.

Read	Trace	Write
went चला गया		
were कर रहे हैं		
what क्या		
when कब		
will मर्जी		
wind हवा		

Read and write the sentence!

went		The crocodile went to the pond.
were		There were lots of toys.
what		What is the lion doing?
when		When are you going to wake up?
will		Will I get it in?
wind		The wind is blowing fiercely.

Read	Trace	Write
wish तमन्ना		
with साथ में		
wood लकड़ी		
work काम		
your तुम्हारी		
about के बारे में		

Read and write the sentence!

wish — I wish you a happy Christmas!

with — He is with his sister.

wood — He is stacking up wooden blocks.

work — He is going to work in his tractor.

your — Your baby is wearing a yellow suit.

about — It's about to be 12:30.

Read
Trace
Write
after
उपरांत
again
फिर
apple
सेब
black
काली
bread
रोटी
bring
लाना

Read and write the sentence!

after		The teacher calmed them after they fought.
again		He did it again!
apple		The apple is red and juicy.
black		The crow is black.
bread		My breakfast is bread and jam.
bring		He is bringing his project.

Read	Trace	Write
brown भूरा		
carry कैरी		
chair कुरसी		
clean स्वच्छ		
could सकता है		
don't नहीं		

Read and write the sentence!

brown	Her stuffed animal is a brown bear.
carry	He is carrying a big crayon.
chair	He is sitting on his chair.
clean	He needs to clean up.
could	The baby could do push-ups.
don't	Don't do that!

Read	Trace	Write
drink पीना		
eight आठ		
every प्रत्येक		
first प्रथम		
floor मंज़िल		
found मिल गया		

drink	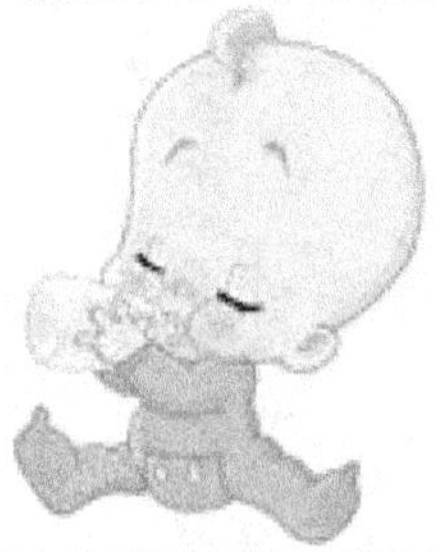	The baby likes to drink water.
eight	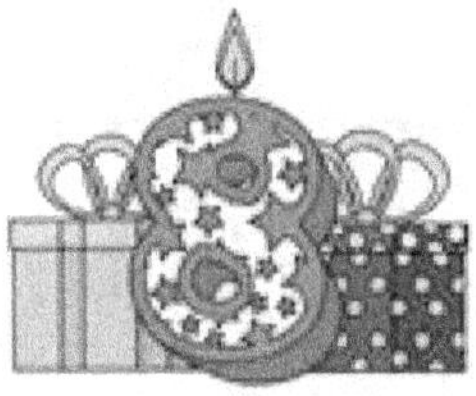	You get eight gifts for turning eight!
every	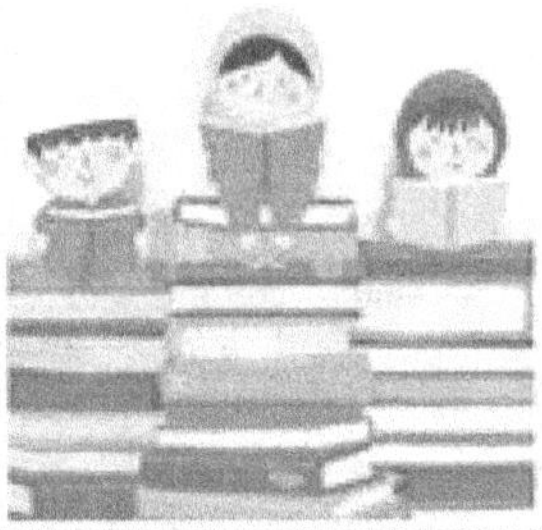	Every book is colorful.
first	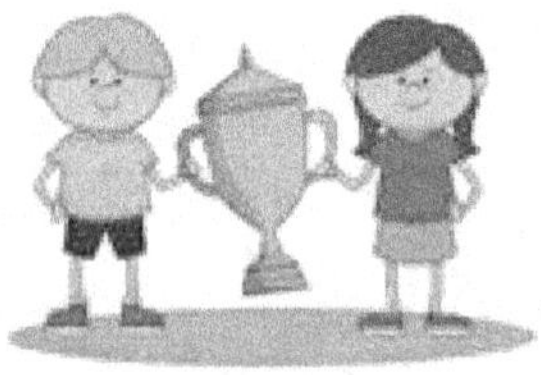	We won first place.
floor	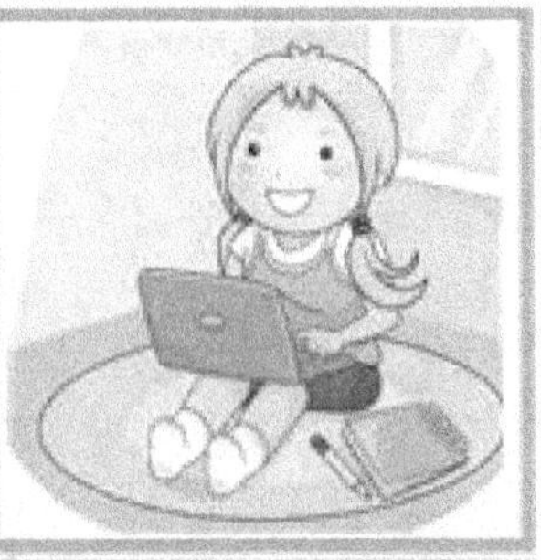	She is sitting on the floor.
found	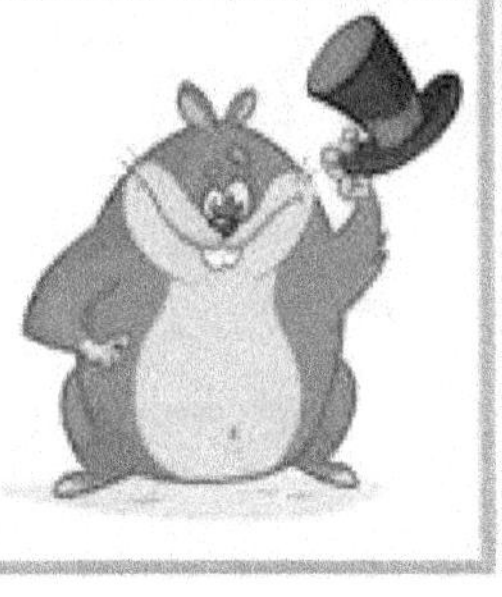	It found a hat in the streets.

Read
Trace
Write

funny
मज़ेदार

going
जाओ

grass
घास

green
हरा

horse
घोड़ा

house
मकान

Read and write the sentence!

funny		The rabbit thinks the joke is funny.
going		The bear is going to eat all the honey.
grass		The goat eats grass on the hill.
green		The turtle that is walking is green.
horse		The horse is magical.
house		They lived in that house.

Read	Trace	Write
kitty बिल्ली		
laugh हसना		
light रोशनी		
money पैसे		
never कभी नहीीं		
night रात		

kitty	The kitties are charming.
laugh	They are laughing while playing.
light	The boy will turn on the lights.
money	I have earned a lot of money.
never	The bear never ate ice cream before.
night	I will sleep on my blanket at night.

Read	Trace	Write
paper कागज़		
party पार्टी		
right सही बात		
round गोल		
seven सात		
shall करेगा		

Read and write the sentence!

paper	I will draw on the paper for a project.
party	The party will be for her birthday.
right	They say we have to go right.
round	The frogs' eyes are round.
seven	The monkey can count to seven.
shall	Shall I make a garden?

Read	Trace	Write
sheep भेड़		
sleep नींद		
small छोटा		
start शुरू		
stick चिपक जाती है		
table तालिका		

sheep	The sheep have a bell around its neck.
sleep	I will go to sleep in my comfortable bed.
small	The small baby will crawl to its crib.
start	She will start sleeping soon.
stick	He has some sticks to play.
table	The table has a toy on it.

Read
Trace
Write
thank
धन्यवाद
their
जो अपने
there
वहाँ
these
इन
thing
चीज़
think
सोच

Read and write the sentence!

thank	He made a Thank you card for you.
their	They will enjoy their picnic.
there	There is something in front of you.
these	These are my eating material.
thing	The thing is broken.
think	She thinks about what she is going to draw.

Read
Trace
Write
those
उन
three
तीन
today
आज
under
के अंतर्गत
watch
घड़ी
water
पानी

Read and write the sentence!

those	Those are mine.
three	She will turn three today.
today	Today is a beautiful day.
under	The puppy sleeps under the blanket.
watch	They both watch the video.
water	He is drinking water after a long soccer game.

Read
Trace
Write

where
कहाँ पे

which
कौन कौन से

white
सफेद

would
चाहेंगे

write
लिखो

always
हमेशा

Read and write the sentence!

where	Where are we?
which	The clothes which are my sisters are colorful.
white	The sheep have white wool.
would	He would tell them a story.
write	I like to write lots of stories.
always	I am always happy that it is Christmas.

Read
Trace
Write

around
चारों ओर

before
इससे पहले

better
बेहतर

farmer
किसान

father
पिता

flower
फूल

Read and write the sentence!

around	I will shuffle the shapes around.
before	Before I go to school, I kiss my mom.
better	I can make it better.
farmer	The farmer takes care of the animals.
father	My father is wearing a blue shirt.
flower	She will play with the flowers.

Read	Trace	Write
garden बगीचा		
ground भूमि		
letter पत्र		
little थोड़ा		
mother मां		
myself खुद		

Read and write the sentence!

garden	Her garden is vast and healthy.
ground	I am playing with my dog on the ground.
letter	These are the letters A, B, and C.
little	The world is small.
mother	My mother is very nice.
myself	I made these by myself.

Read	Trace	Write
please कृप्या		
pretty सुंदर		
rabbit खरगोश		
school स्कूल		
sister बहन		
street सड़क		

please	Please stop pulling my hair.
pretty	She made the cake very pretty.
rabbit	The rabbit is white and soft.
school	This is the school.
sister	My sister is wearing a pink dress.
street	They are walking across the street.

Read	Trace	Write
window खिड़की		
yellow पीला		
because चूंकि		
brother भाई		
chicken मुर्गी		
goodbye अलविदा		

Read and write the sentence!

window

The window is open.

yellow

The ducky is yellow.

because

She will sleep because it is night.

brother

His brother is playing with him.

chicken

The chicken has hatched out of the egg.

goodbye

The animal is saying goodbye.

Read	Trace	Write
morning सुबह		
picture चित्र		
birthday जन्मदिन		
children बच्चे		
squirrel गिलहरी		
together साथ में		

Read and write the sentence!

morning	He likes to ride his bike in the morning.
picture	He will take a picture.
birthday	Today is my birthday!
children	The children are doing something.
squirrel	The squirrel is cute.
together	They are sharing a bed together.

www.ingramcontent.com/pod-product-compliance
Lightning Source LLC
Chambersburg PA
CBHW081350160726
48000CB00010B/3276